MW01100894

To _____

Trust

From _____

Trust

Illustrated by
JUDY PELIKAN

A Welcome Book

Stewart, Tabori & Chang
Publishers, New York

Published in 1994 and distributed in the U.S. by
Stewart, Tabori & Chang, 575 Broadway,
New York, New York 10012

Produced by Welcome Enterprises, Inc.
575 Broadway, New York, New York 10012
Text Research: Sally Seamans, Shannon Rothenberger

1 3 5 7 9 10 8 6 4 2
Printed in Italy

*Grateful acknowledgment is made to the following for permission to
reprint previously published material:*

Excerpt from *Zorba the Greek* by Nikos Kazantzakis. Copyright
© 1953 by Simon & Schuster, Inc. Copyright Renewed © 1981
by Simon & Schuster, Inc. Reprinted by Permission of Simon
& Schuster, Inc.

Traditional Chinese Tale from *Chinese Fairy Tales and Fantasies*
by Moss Roberts. Copyright © 1979 by Moss Roberts.
Reprinted by permission of Pantheon Books, a division of
Random House, Inc.

David Ignatow, "With the Door Open" reprinted from *Selected
Poems* © 1975 by Wesleyan University. By permission of
University Press of New England.

"Trust Me" by Jean Valentine. Reprinted by permission of
the author.

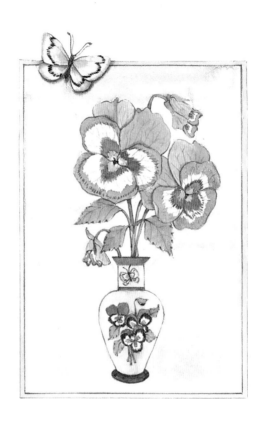

THOSE

who trust us educate us.

GEORGE ELIOT

came down from the hillock and lay on the cool pebbles. There was a light breeze, the sea was faintly ruffled; two seagulls bobbed up and down on the tiny waves, with necks fluffed out, voluptuously enjoying the movement of the water.

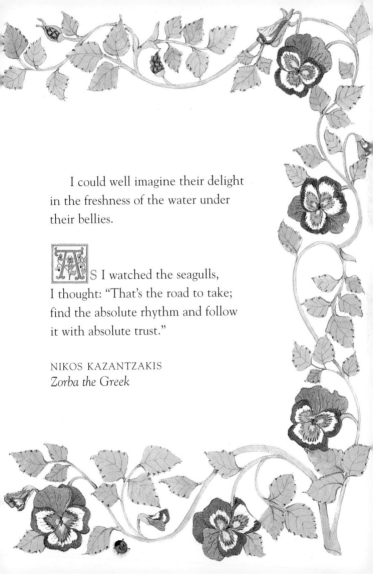

I could well imagine their delight
in the freshness of the water under
their bellies.

AS I watched the seagulls,
I thought: "That's the road to take;
find the absolute rhythm and follow
it with absolute trust."

NIKOS KAZANTZAKIS
Zorba the Greek

World, thou choosest not the better part!
It is not wisdom to be only wise,
And on the inward vision close the eyes,
But it is wisdom to believe the heart.

COLUMBUS found a world, and
　　had no chart,
Save one that faith deciphered in the skies;

To trust the soul's invincible surmise
Was all his science and his only art.

GEORGE SANTAYANA
O World, Thou Choosest Not

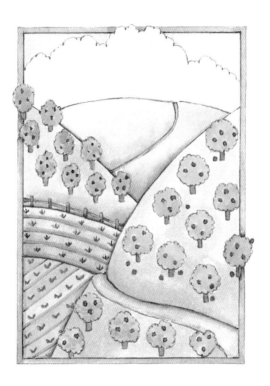

man whose axe was missing suspected his neighbor's son. The boy walked like a thief, looked like a thief, and spoke like a thief. But the man found his axe while he was digging in the valley, and the next time he saw his neighbor's son, the boy walked, looked, and spoke like any other child.

TRADITIONAL CHINESE TALE

OMETHING

I want to communicate to you,
I keep my door open between us.
I am unable to say it,
I am happy only
with the door open between us.

DAVID IGNATOW
With the Door Open

TRUST

men, and they will be true to you;
treat them greatly, and they will show
themselves great.

RALPH WALDO EMERSON
On Prudence

TRUST
one who has gone through it.

VIRGIL
Aeneid

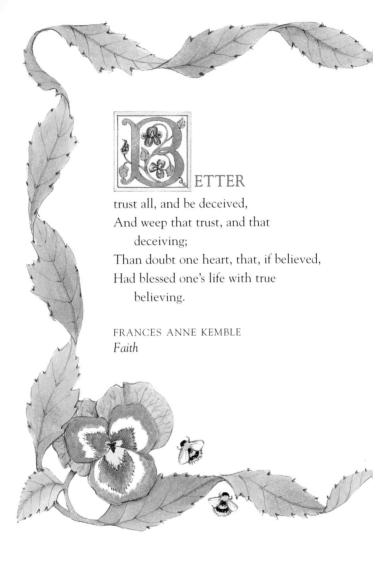

BETTER
trust all, and be deceived,
And weep that trust, and that
    deceiving;
Than doubt one heart, that, if believed,
Had blessed one's life with true
    believing.

FRANCES ANNE KEMBLE
Faith

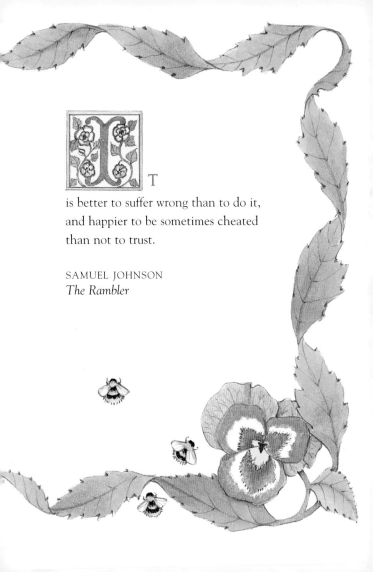

IT
is better to suffer wrong than to do it,
and happier to be sometimes cheated
than not to trust.

SAMUEL JOHNSON
The Rambler

WHO

did I write last night? leaning
over this yellow pad, here, inside,
making blue chicken tracks: two
sets of blue footprints, tracking out
on a yellow ground,
child's colors.

Who am I?
who want so much to move
like a fish through water,
through life . . .

               Fish *like* to be

underwater.

Fish move through fish! Who
are you?

AND Trust Me said, There's
    another way to go,
we'll go by the river which is frozen
    under the snow;

my shining, your shining life draws
    close, draws closer,
God fills us as a woman fills a pitcher.

JEAN VALENTINE
Trust Me

E

like the bird, who
Halting in his flight
On limb too slight
Feels it give way beneath him,
Yet sings
Knowing he hath wings.

VICTOR HUGO

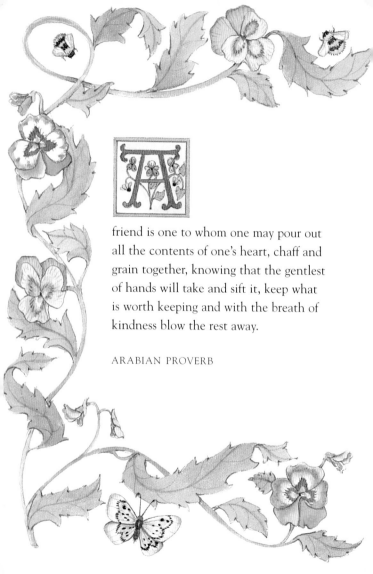

A friend is one to whom one may pour out all the contents of one's heart, chaff and grain together, knowing that the gentlest of hands will take and sift it, keep what is worth keeping and with the breath of kindness blow the rest away.

ARABIAN PROVERB

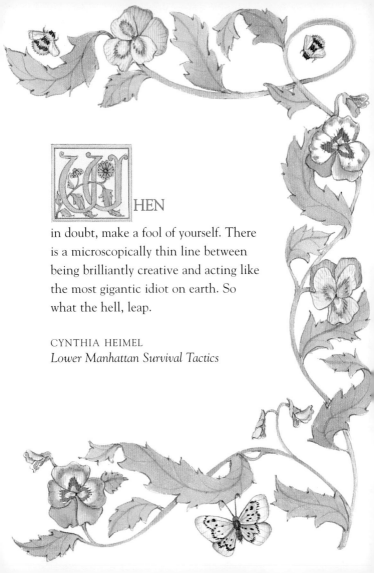

WHEN

in doubt, make a fool of yourself. There is a microscopically thin line between being brilliantly creative and acting like the most gigantic idiot on earth. So what the hell, leap.

CYNTHIA HEIMEL
Lower Manhattan Survival Tactics

N

old man whose black face
shines golden-brown as wet pebbles
under the streetlamp, is walking
two mongrel dogs of dis-
proportionate size, in the rain,
in the relaxed early-evening avenue.

The small sleek one wants to stop,
docile to the imploring soul of the
      trashbasket,
but the young tall curly one
wants to walk on; the glistening sidewalk
entices him to arcane happenings.

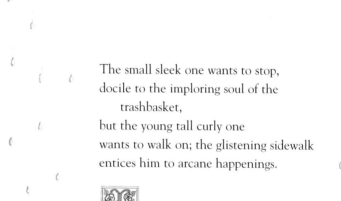

INCREASING rain. The old
bareheaded man smiles and grumbles to
      himself.
The lights change: the avenue's
endless nave echoes notes of
liturgical red. He drifts

between his dogs' desires.
The three of them are enveloped—
turning now to go crosstown—in their
sense of each other, of pleasure,
of weather, of corners,
of leisurely tensions between them
and private silence.

DENISE LEVERTOV
The Rainwalkers

We are not lovers
because of the love
we make
but the love
we have

We are not friends
because of the laughs
we spend
but the tears
we save

I don't want to be near you
for the thoughts we share
but the words we never have
to speak

I will never miss you
because of what we do
but what we are
together

NIKKI GIOVANNI
A Poem of Friendship

FEAR
knocked at the door.
Faith answered.
There was no one there.

On a sign over an old inn
Bray, England

I am simply on the earth.
Need I be afraid?

HIDATSA INDIAN SONG

WHEN

we are going toward someone we say
you are just like me
your thoughts are my brothers and sisters
word matches word
how easy to be together.

When we are leaving someone we say
how strange you are
we cannot communicate
we can never agree
how hard, hard and weary to be together.

We are not different nor alike
but each strange in our leather bodies
sealed in skin and reaching out clumsy
    hands
and loving is an act
that cannot outlive
the open hand
the open eye
the door in the chest standing open.

MARGE PIERCY
Simple-Song

let it go—the
smashed word broken
open vow or
the oath cracked length
wise—let it go it
was sworn to
        go

let them go—the
truthful liars and
the false fair friends
and the boths and
neithers—you must let them go they
were born
        to go

let all go—the
big small middling
tall bigger really
the biggest and all
things—let all go
dear

    so comes love

E. E. CUMMINGS
let it go—the

learned this, at least . . . that if one advances confidently in the direction of his dreams, and endeavors to live the life which he has imagined, he will meet with a success unexpected in common hours. . . . In proportion as he simplifies his life, the laws of the universe will appear less complex, and solitude will not be solitude, nor poverty poverty, nor weakness weakness.

HENRY DAVID THOREAU
Walden

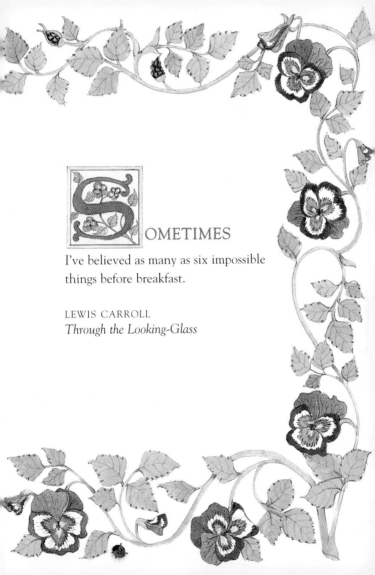

SOMETIMES

I've believed as many as six impossible
things before breakfast.

LEWIS CARROLL
Through the Looking-Glass

EY,

this little kid gets roller skates.
She puts them on.
She stands up and almost
flops over backwards.
She sticks out a foot like
she's going somewhere and
falls down and
smacks her hand. She
grabs hold of a step to get up and
sticks out the other foot and
slides about six inches and
falls and
skins her knee.

ND then, you know what?

SHE brushes off the dirt and the
blood and puts some
spit on it and then
sticks out the other foot

   again.

MYRA COHN LIVINGSTON
74th Street

T
was growing dark on this long southern
evening and suddenly, at the exact point
her finger had indicated, the moon lifted
a forehead of stunning gold above the
horizon, lifted straight out of filigreed,
light-intoxicated clouds that lay on the
skyline in attendant veils. Behind us,
the sun was setting in a simultaneous
congruent withdrawal and the river turned
to flame in a quiet duel of gold. . . .

THE new gold of moon astonishing and ascendant, the depleted gold of sunset extinguishing itself in the long westward slide, it was the old dance of days in the Carolina marshes, the breathtaking death of days before the eyes of children, until the sun vanished, its final signature a ribbon of bullion strung across the tops of water oaks. The moon then rose quickly, rose like a bird from the water, from the trees, from the islands, and climbed straight up—gold, then yellow, then pale yellow, pale silver, silver-bright, then something miraculous, immaculate, and beyond silver, a color native only to southern nights.

E children sat transfixed before that moon our mother had called forth from the waters. When the moon had reached its deepest silver, my sister, Savannah, though only three, cried aloud to our mother, to Luke and me, to the river and the moon, "Oh, Mama, do it again!"

PAT CONROY
The Prince of Tides

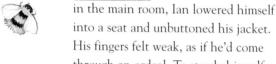

OUT
in the main room, Ian lowered himself
into a seat and unbuttoned his jacket.
His fingers felt weak, as if he'd come
through an ordeal. To steady himself,
he bowed his head and prayed.

H E prayed as he almost always did, not forming actual words but picturing instead this spinning green planet safe in the hands of God, with the children and his parents and Ian himself small trusting dots among all the other dots. And the room around him seemed to rustle with prayers from years and years past: *Let me get well* and *Make her love me* and *Forgive what I have done*.

ANNE TYLER
Saint Maybe

UST trust yourself, then you will know how to live.

JOHANN WOLFGANG VON GOETHE